UNCIVILIZING

UNCIVILIZING

INSOMNIAC PRESS

Edited by Jennifer Footman
Copy edited by Caroline H. Davidson and Mike O'Connor
Designed by Mike O'Connor

Canadian Cataloguing in Publication Data

Main entry under title:

Uncivilizing

ISBN 1-895837-17-0

1. Canadian poetry (English) - 20th century - *
I. Footman, Jennifer, 1942-   .

PS8293.U52 1997   C811'.5408   C97-931371-6
PR9195.7.U52 1997

Printed and bound in Canada

The publisher gratefully acknowledges the support of the Ontario Arts Council.

Insomniac Press
378 Delaware Ave.
Toronto, Ontario, Canada, M6H 2T8

to all our fantastic families and fans

Contents

INTRODUCTION

Adult is a dirty word, a word to be catalogued with the other dirty words like sex, chocolate, intellectual, mature, polite, considerate, well-mannered and of course, the three well known four-letter Anglo-Saxon words.

Warning: Adult content. Danger: Mature theme. Peril: erotic material. Caution: intellectual activity required.

'New and exciting' is more or less synonymous with 'young' in today's media jargon. If a poet is exciting she\he has to be young, and when the word NEW is used about a poet, we know he\she can be no older than twenty-odd. Poetry groups promote the new, exciting and thrilling.

Goodness. None of these six poets is young. Not one is under thirty! Well, they can't be interesting, can they? Has been's? Or never been's? Over the hill. Done in. Done for. Been there, done that.

Well, beware, there is indeed mature content here. Content which makes a reader think, makes a reader work, changes a reader and excites a reader.

We have four well-established, not young poets here: Roger Nash, Robert Sward, Bernice Lever and James Reaney. Added to them are two newer mature voices: Sonja Dunn and Caroline Davidson.

These are all men and women who have found their voices. They are certain, in an adult way, about the things they are saying. Their work is honed and polished just as their lives are honed and polished. There comes a time in any intelligent person's life when he\she has to know where one is and where one is going. There are no doubts here; there are no indulgences requested; there is no self-pity; here adults talk to adults. They know what they are doing and do it superbly well.

I feel that all the poems say something, and that's a rarity in itself in this day of waffle and 'so what' poems.

But I am biased. My own taste in poetry leans towards the passionate, the finished, the crafted, the honed, the deeply felt, the mature, the serious, the humorous, and the ironic.

Diane Wakoski said, when accused of being elitist, "Hell no, anyone can join my club. I exclude no one. Anyone can join. They just have to do a bit of work."

Not that I'm implying that these poems are obscure. Rather most of them are accessible on one level, but enrich the reader even more if one is prepared to work at them.

It was a great pleasure working on this collection. A pleasure and an honour. Reading through the work I felt I got to know the poets and entered their worlds. I am a very lucky person.

Jennifer Footman, Editor

Jennifer Footman, born in India, raised in Edinburgh, runs workshops and Brampton Writers' Guild. President of Canadian Poetry Association, she writes both prose and poetry. Her third poetry book was St.Valentine's Day (Broken Jaw Press, 1995).

BERNICE LEVER

BERNICE LEVER, poet and prose writer, now lives in Richmond Hill, Ontario and teaches English at Seneca College. Active in the League of Canadian Poets, Canadian Authors Association, and Canadian Poetry Association, her work has appeared in a dozen anthologies; she has published over 200 short pieces and 6 books of poetry.

From 1972-1987, she edited WAVES, a literary magazine. Since1967, she has coordinated the Richvale Writers Club, and made listeners of her readings in Canada, Japan, Australia, England and U.S.A. laugh and cry. After her grammar text and healing chants, she looks forward to retiring to Sechelt on the west coast. EMAIL: bfarrar@learn.senecac.on.ca
Website: http://learn.senecac.on.ca/~bfarrar/

WE BREATHE ONLY OXYGEN

Trees are dying; to the north acid rain is eating them.
    They can't inhale much of our exhaust.
Every year more people are breathing more O_2;
        every year more babies are exhaling CO_2.
Trees are being cut, de-limbed, de-barked,
        even drowned in hydro projects,
        even their roots are ploughed up and out.
Every year, fewer of them producing O_2.
        They need more than our good breath — CO_2;
        they need clean rain and fertile earth.
We keep breathing, and creating more babies;
        we only breathe by the gift of their breath.
Every minute: a giant cedar crashes down
        on the soggy west coast,
        rusty bark as thick as your wrist
        but no longer alive as your lungs.
Every minute — falling — faster, ever faster:
        a moss covered cypress, a flowering magnolia
        a pitch sticky pine, a lush bread fruit tree.
Every minute — here — there — birds flap off
        as ground squirrels scurry — where?
        as fish gasp in ash laden waters
            while wild flowers fry
        from the heat of burning stumps.
Countries of lifeless grey and black skeleton trees.
Every year more trees are disappearing;
        fewer are exhaling oxygen;
            more of us —
                fewer of them —
yet we only breathe by the gift of their breath.
Trees are dying;
        our turn is coming.

A TARGET

It's happened;
anyone can tell you, there is a plot:
just listen to the gossip, snide asides, innuendos,
a smear campaign is smudging my name.
I'm disappearing,
soon no one will admit
to ever have known me.

My enemies have a plan:
writs, liens, lawsuits attack
my dwindling dollar deals,
properties flooded, and buildings burned
until my assets are in ashes.

I'm the target;
these plotters have marked me:
a bull's eye painted on my shoulder blades
an apple balances on my head
my shoes are filled with plastic explosive
            ready for the first time I stamp in anger
trip wires are set for the next time
            I open that marked door
so nitro will splash on my face˙
            or shiny guillotine will slice my neck.

I am replaceable. I am expendable.
   Start playing target practice
   as the line forms to the right!

TOMORROW I WILL STEAL A BLACKJACK

I will wear my red nylon ski mitts
— you never leave your fingerprints
on the murder weapon.
I have a list of possible candidates:
am just devising criteria
or priorities for which of you
should be first, after all,
being my first victim
should be an honour in itself.
Who wants a no-name killer,
just a run-of-the-mill mugger
who eliminated you
for being at the right place
at the wrong time?

Death by a celebrity's hand
is so much better,
high profile trials
will allow the media to highlight
every aspect and ash of your existence,
your passing will be dramatized
for TV and serialized for radio,
if talk show hosts should mouth you
to death, an original cause
makes your body a cause célèbre —
black jacked!

Being struck dumb by a pack of cards,
being left to freeze naked
in a snow field in an Ontario January blizzard,
just these sets of cards adding to twenty-one
stuck under limbs — here & there —
just jack of all trades
being hijacked out of life,

not even a proper metal,
that black steel blackjack
to pound your brains into submission —
now no car jack will lift you into breathing,
you're just a stiff cream form
in a farmer's white field,
waiting for your 15 seconds of fame
on the local evening news, until blackout
unable to make the major leagues
of a 15 minute magazine piece on national TV —
but I will as all my past lovers
ignore my red ski mitts
and identify my nude body walking into town,
looking for that microphone
and the cameras, to tell my story.

BEWARE PASSION, MY FRIEND

Your words pour passion
burning listening ears
until minds warm and whimper
hearts flare and flame

you become their life source
as they flock to your feet
to catch that lava
— searing against injustices —
from your impudent lips

you scorch their enemies
while burying their fears
in fire, ash and pumice;
your words hot-wire their wholeness

with gasping lungs and heated bodies
they swarm you wanting
just to feel your fiery surface,
as if one touch could alight them
as if creativity is contagious

as circling arms and legs
of those adoring trip your dancing steps
          you hot-footing it over boiling waters
until you join the choicest openings offered
— the finest matched ember
          or even promised moment's coolness —
only to discover fans are vampires
          and lips once melted together are silent

spent in flesh, the performer lies
          wordless

THIS LADY
a Cautious Woman — downstairs in that bar

This Lady: she'll think and be alive,
        she don't drink and drive,
        she don't drink and fuck,
        so buddy, you're out of luck!

"Let's have a beer and talk."
was his sly offer and
accepted at face value,
thus saving face and ass all round
between rounds of tasteless froth.

    a Cautious Woman — upstairs in his room

Somehow I couldn't see myself:
eating tinned salmon sandwiches and
drinking scotch with warm water
from dribbling bathroom taps or
fucking on this faded flowered bedspread
in this sleazy hotel room
with its gasping air conditioner
        almost silencing
the bleating of city taxis and
gnawing of unknown bugs and
all those guffawing men
in the bar three floors below —

Talk of Helen of Troy! here
all my face was launching was
        one aging poet
on a short fantasy
that fans were flesh
lusting after his.

EATING

With my fistful of cents-off coupons,
I enter the automatic doors
in anticipation;
today I'll find a satisfying bargain,
a perfect fit
for my taste and budget.
Gluttony feeds my imagination,
while the offered 'deals of the week'
starve my body.
"Save! save! save!" But what is safe?

Eat, eating, ate, have been eaten:
pleasure all over now
as I am attracted
by every forbidden fruit of the 90's.
Supermarket shelves seem to be showing
row after row of enticing foods:
tempting Italian sausages — too high in cholesterol,
lush Hawaiian pineapple with too much fibre,
delicious dark chocolate torte hiding its sugar,
Mexican salsa chip dip — too spicy for my ulcers,
crusty long sticks of French bread
suggesting the starch was baked out of them,
crisp cucumber and salad pals
pretending they grew without pesticides,
and all those amazing claims of low-cal
supermarket alcohol don't raise my spirits.

I keep busy, pushing my empty basket,
searching for suitable food;
I can count calories,
but I can't remove the additives.

Yet I have my feasting memories
when everything was chosen for delight,
when taste was all that counted,
memories of your tongue and lips,
your hands and other things
eating.

SCARCE AS ANGELS

Don't arrive printed
with a big capital 'O' stamped
clearly on their foreheads
  with simultaneous translation
  as the question to pursue —

We've progressed
beyond 'A' for adultery
  Hawthorne deciphered that Puritan burr
that negative label that silenced
  the next 25 symbols —
poor old 'O' more than half way down
  the winning stretch to eternity —
is usually only classified
  codified and recorded in history
  as under 'missed opportunities'.

What clues are there in the eye of the beholder
or the handshake of a friend of a friend
  on a blind date with your mask to decode as
"Oh, this is the big 'O' ? "

Opportunities are as scarce as angels
  but with better disguises,
creative chameleons
whimsical bastards that tantalize us
  from the other side of the dance floor,
we see their movements, a bit of shape
  through the rhythmic limbs that separate us —
in our eagerness, our desperate despairing,
we clutch at any round symbol or cycle,
believing that it is 'O' —
  yes, our completion,

our mouths struggling for that perfect oval
        as we lock in embraces,
surely, this one, this time,
this 'O' ,

     o   OO   oo
                      O

Hurting You

Hurting you was never
part of my plan
I never meant,
        "You're always a loser."
what I said was,
        "This proves you don't have a brain.
        I mean not checking the gas level!"
This doesn't mean that
I was trying to hurt you,
it was just something I had to do,
blurt out words for my own relief.

I never meant to hurt you,
but saying "sorry" never helps,
        is no excuse nor solution.
Sorry is a useless band-aid
always slipping off and
never helping to heal hurt.

What I said wasn't intended
        to hurt you,
it wasn't directed at
        you personally,
just things can go wrong at cottages.
Just a passing observation
that I did mean,
        "Remember, I was the one in labour
        in a boat out of gas!"
well, but not to be painful.

I never meant to hurt you
at first   but now
I do, I do!

HEART-TO-HEART TALKING

Please, little pump keep pumping
fat-laden, rusting blood
through this aging body

these cooling hands and feet
need your fresh heaters:
those oxygen fuel cells

kidneys and liver struggle
waiting for you, dear heart
to suck away their wastes
to replenish their food shelves

stomach full, even distended
begs your engine's flow to power
its digestion and digressions

fainting senses and sensibilities
plead for the smelling salts
of your life-line liquor
as you feed energy to my climaxes

your beats: the most precious music
Oh heart, know you are loved.

HEART COMPLAINS

Just spare me a beat, bubba!
You think you have any
      pulse without me?

Talk about taking my name
in vain, oh, your vanity
is without horizon
tho' I can make you horizontal!

'Heartless' you whine, and what do
you know about being without me?
      You wouldn't be at all,
you — a self-inflated body —
calling yourself 'hearty'!

You mock me, making me a plaything
with clubs and spades and diamonds;
then give a solitaire
to your 'heart's desire'
without asking me if I agree.

You encourage cannibalism
as you urge the envious
"to eat your heart out".
Thanks bubba, why not offer a big toe,
especially the one with the ingrown nail!

Just leave me out of your mixed
metaphors, oh talking head!
      Why not, 'the brain of the matter'
'learn by nose' 'take knees' 'have a spleen'
'eye ache' 'stomach broken' 'bum sick'
or 'it does my belly button good' ?
When you demand that I keep
contracting and dilating,
you just remember
I hold the contract
      on when you die.

Heart Talks Back

Endless demands
with sillier cheer leading chants,
        go man go
fight woman fight

well, give me a break!
        you need this area sent
white cells for repair
        but others sent as infection
fighters somewhere else

here and there, you know,
the opposite ends of this
mis-used mangle of muscle and bone
you call your body;
it's easy for you
you just give commands, orders,
I'm the one that has to do the work!

next, it's your arms and legs
demanding bright red oxygen
rich energy supplies
for those trendy aerobic classes
while your smoke and smog clogged lungs
play work-to-rule games

well, I've got tougher muscles
than you'll ever see on those sweaty limbs
as you punish me in the sauna
or worse, in shell-shock Polar Bear swims

don't ask me to calm your self—
induced stress, how many hours of sleep
do I get? never even a forty wink cat nap
and holidays, forget them
they're just another endurance test, for me
as you quick dry brains with Margaritas,
sun sear your surface and then expect me

to help you impress some special sexy
senor or senorita!
   You can save your whining praises,
too late for words, no sweet syllables can repair
the damage of your temper tantrums punching me,
especially not after all the junk food you expect
me to survive on!
   my valves snap in anger
at the way you abuse me,
there ought'a be a law against...

'THEY'

They smiled
when they splashed me
in mud puddles

They grinned
when they dumped me
in garbage bins

They laughed loudly
when they dropped me
head first down
that outhouse hole

Then I was small
      and they were big

Then I was weak
      and they were wrong

But only in muscle and bone
my spirit was never alone
      others washed me in tears
      clean hands held mine
and the Lord answered my painful prayers.

Now I am healing, my scars are fading
      and I pity them
as the child is remembered with love
by the adult self: a hand in a well-worn glove.

TOMBSTONES

Advertising for the dead:
who's buying
and who's selling
reputations by the phrase?

More scanned
than Life magazine,

most leave wilted
forget-me-nots;

few take the stone
verses home.

Who's listening
and who's telling
that James T. Jones
one hundred years ago
was good at it?

THIS BIRD WITH THE BULLET IN ITS BILL

Red-breasted, white throated,
lime-green feathered,
this bird flies off
with the metal evidence.

Tough and tropical, the Jacamar
is said to eat buzzing
honey bees for appetizers.

This long white beak
like a bony gun barrel
crunches soft wasp bodies
in half, each mouth-sized
morsel swallowed whole.

Like magpies drawn by shine,
perhaps the Jacamar
was intrigued by the blood
on the silver cylinder.

It's just a sidebar
mystery to what occurred
after the lethal shot
as birds usually tell all,
not hide the music.

'HOW YA BEN?'
— *for Carol Malyon*

"Lousy, can't get out of this soap opera
I'm in — just splashing around in tear
jerking suds called the bath of life."

Let's swap stories; our fantasies
must be better than our lives,
or we wouldn't be forced to create
such fictions, giving ourselves
an element of control,
shaping beginnings & endings,
we'll pretend a shape that is
not found in the endless
splotches of our lives —

Let's just hug, accept & praise
each other; why try to interpret
a dozen — or even a six pack —
of annual family disasters
that seem pale parlour jokes
now that they are over,
no longer looming as life threatening.

"How ya ben? Lousy: felt
lost & unloved coast to coast or
seemed adored from Halifax to Victoria,
depends on my season, which day you ask!"

CAROLINE H. DAVIDSON

CAROLINE H. DAVIDSON, of Pickering, Ontario, grew up in Ithaca, New York. Her father was a physicist and her mother an artist who gave her an imagistic eye and unlimited atoms to read. Mostly for the fun of it, she has been writing since high school.

Her work has been published in anthologies, magazines and newspapers. Caroline is a wife, mother and grandmother with a day job as purchasing agent for a manufacturer. When not singing choir solos, her good 'ear' collects bits of fascinating conversations. Beware!

BILLY

She walks toward me
in the hot sunlight
away from where
her brother lies
suddenly broken
impatient activity tamed.
Wind blows her dress gently
as she walks, arm wrapped
around her living love
strong shoulders, red beard.

I take her limp hand
Billy's face bright in my eyes
"There's nothing you can say."
Her voice echoes voices
grief words murmured
between women in dark dresses
standing in hot, stony fields
holding folded hands.

MISSING

In the warm haze
of after-dinner Spanish coffee
we see a poster with six faces
eager young laughing
high school photos
of life just beginning

MISSING, HAVE YOU SEEN...
SEARCHED, TO NO AVAIL...

Reminds me of spring '95
of ominous rumbling
Rat tat tat tat
yellow and red helicopter
hovering over the shoreline
passing near my house
windows and eaves rattling
moving slowly back again
its shadow covering
every wavelet and stone
hopefully searching for those
who will never come home

SIMON RECORDING FOR HIS GREAT-GRANDMOTHER
Nov. 6, 1995

Simon sits on the piano bench
stretches a shoe to reach the pedal
I start the machine to record
for the great-grandmother
we visit on Friday
"I am going to play Study #9"
fingers poised, he wiggles
then plays the first notes.

Sound swells out around his body
black notes on white paper
translated by fingers to strings
sounding board vibrations
bring Beethoven's song to this room
swell my heart with joy
record this grandchild's fun
for my mother to listen.

Fingers dancing on keys
remind me of my father's
short fat fingers delicately
creating music to dream by
my sister and I snuggled
between cedar wool blankets
could see his swaying shadow
as he played our bedtime concert.

His red hair long gone
gleams again on Simon's head
bobbing over the keyboard
as fingers riff to a pounding climax.
I press Stop, Rewind and Play.
We listen to recorded joy
encapsulated in this black box
to be opened and shared in a distant room.

MOON ON THE RISE

After the long drive north
Noise of the week receding
Pull the canoe to water
Load in the food and wine

Lift,
Dip the paddle deeply
Pushing away from shore
Dreams of our little cabin
You waiting by the door

Lift,
Dip the paddle homeward
Home to the place we chose
Tall trees whispering
Water lapping stones

Lift,
Dip the paddle homeward
Working the wood and hammers
Building the house together
Growing our love for each other

Lift,
Thrust the paddle deeply
Push for the moonlit channel
Toward the tall tree spire
Close by our floating dock

Lift,
Thrust the paddle faster
Pushing it down in the deep
Home to the fire warming
Home to the love in your eyes

My Grandfather's Eye

My grandfather's eye
is like the swamp
clumps of dried grass
with dark wet places in between

Through the cloudy white sieve
of his ancient cataract
he looks into my mind
examines every tiny idea
sees all my faults
carefully explains them to me

When I was in the swamp
as a little child in big boots
the murky mud grabbed
my rubber bound legs
tried to hold me down
I slipped my feet out
and ran away in my socks

THE CONTEST

The contest begins
across an elegant table
You,
pouring on the lines.
     I,
having heard them before.
You could sell bronzed baby shoes
to my grandmother
a Fiat to Henry Ford
but the snow falls softly
in delicate patterns
wrapping my shoulders
in white Irish lace
of tenderness and fun.
I accept the challenge
and start knitting in grey
a thick woolly muffler
to warm up the snowman

MAMA HELEN

Through the small end of the telescope
I look back forty years
to your favourite aunt
her smooth grey cap of hair
so like yours now

In that room were old notebooks
with your poems
in decorative writing
quiet metered lines
now you read my poems

Your warm smooth fingers
settle on mine
I feel your gnarled knuckles
with no rings
remember the bulging veins
on the backs of your hands
that fascinated me
in our sunlit kitchen

Today you give me your pearl ring
that you always wore at dinner
I put it on and see
my brown spots, bulging veins
my hand is yours.

SPLITTING ROCKS

At the beach splitting rocks
loud waves crash beside us
run up the small stones
wash around boulders.

We look for pieces of shale
oblongs of soft dark grey
hold them on edge against a boulder
gently tapping along the top.

Cracks appear and widen
he carefully pries the layers
parts these rocky pages
revealing dark wet textures
luminous bones of creatures.

Long ago, before Christ
before Gilgamesh
they slithered into warm mud
nuzzled shadowy cousins
drifted into murky darkness of sleep.

Shiny sardine bones
exposed today under the same sun
my fingers trace a body
no human ever touched.

THE SUMMER BARN

The weathered dark red paint
echoes with chatter of sparrows
nesting among the green leaves
of grapevines that crawl up
the cracked wooden walls.

We walk into the dusky cool
carefully stepping around the splats
on the ground below the swallow's nest
a continuing annoyance to Father
who parks the family car in this spot.

In the dim mustiness lurk
treasures from long ago
when Grandfather was a boy
curved iron structures for dairy stalls
that we use for climbing gyms.

Under a fly-specked window
on a broken chair half-buried
in the dusty hay and cobwebs
is a small filing cabinet
walnut drawers full of postcards
from places in Africa,
South America and Hawaii.

Far down at the end is a pen
full of Grandfather's Rhode Island Red hens
and one rooster and a large pan of water.
My sister picks up a corn cob
reaches through the wire
winks at me and carefully aims.

She throws — the rooster jumps
right into the water in the pan
and up out the other side
shakes his feathers and runs
screeching crossly after three hens.

We laugh hysterically
doubled over in the dust
then fear of our Grandfather
makes us run down the length
to the wide open door
sunlight and sparrows.

PENELOPE

Practical Penelope
I ask for your guidance
as I wait at my window
for my somewhere king.
You parried advances
of mediocre suitors
and kept your serenity
calm and desirable.
Teach me the secrets
of the beauty of your soul
that I may be patient
weaving my pattern,
hoping that tomorrow
will bring to my kitchen
the smell of salt sea-weed
and Odysseus, disguised.

PENELOPE'S MONOLOGUE

Not know you, Odysseus?
The smell of your skin
your eyes of amber fire?
After ten years of longing for
the roughness of those calloused fingers
on my warm places.
Years of weaving
while those young boys
breathed their wet dreams
on my opals
their avaricious teeth ready
to gobble my wealth.

Not know you?
Slurping soup in my kitchen
like an old beggar,
Athena adorns in the silver of old age
but she can not hide the fire
that gleams from your eyes
the steel muscles
rippling grey hairs on your arms.

So, you sneak into my kitchen
question my faithfulness?
After those long nights of un-weaving
my body aching
my embers darkening
without your fire.
I'll wait 'til tomorrow
to show you my joy.

VARIATION ON A THEME OF EROS

There was the time
he mailed the shopping list
    Didn't you, Joe
    Yes, Marion

He had a letter to our Peggy
all the stamps and everything
He was just day-dreaming
        Weren't you, Joe
            Just dreaming, Marion

Dropped the shopping list
in the box, didn't you, Joe
           You know I did, Marion

Then he went to Marvin's Deli
and gave them the letter
He said, "Pack up this stuff for me
I'll be back in half an hour"
and he went to the fishing goods store
      Right, Joe?
          You bet, Marion

When he came back, Marvin said
"What stuff did you want, Joe?
This letter says Peggy
not Piggy; Piggies I have
chops and tenderloin
Your Peggy married someone else."
      Remember, Joe?
          You know I do, Marion

Now, Marvin asks about Peggy
every time you go there
     Doesn't he, Joe?
         Yes, Marion

He mailed the letter
on the way home
but he couldn't remember
what was on the list
     Could you, Joe?

So you had to come home
to ask me
     Didn't you, Joe
         Yes, Marion

PUPPETEER

She says she makes him
do what she wants.

Is he a puppet dangling
on a string?
Bump-bumping against her
chest hairs tickling breasts
hard parts touching soft.

Does she pull the string
jiggling and tickling
'til her excitement builds
rises to climax
then pushes him away
done for the night
or week?

Can I tug-tug on your string
inflame the hot places
control the program?

But where is the fun?
The surprise of your choice
wanting me now
offering me pleasure
propelling me to thrills
our joyous responses.

WHERE IS IT WRITTEN?

Where is it written
that wives get to go to work
and men get to stay home
and only do the cooking
and the vacuuming
and the laundry
and take the cat to the vet?

Where is it written
that wives get the factory bullshit
and make long explanations
for somebody else's mistakes
and send back all the stuff
that was ordered incorrectly
and men get to stay home
and discourse with the furnace man   five times
and check on the roof repair man
and make sure the water is delivered
and mow the lawn?

Where is it written
that wives over fifty
should have the good jobs
and be independent
and stressed out
and men over fifty
should be out of work
and be dependent
and go to parties where they meet
other men over fifty also out of work
with stressed out wives?

NEIGHBOURS

I tells 'er, I does
I says, You fence up them dogs
so's they don't dump their lumps
on my yard.

I can't be always pickin' up
their lumps when I's mowin'
this 'ere grass.

I wants me grass to look nice
an' it does!
But them pups leaves their lumps in it
makes me mad.

I tells 'er, I did.

WHILE DAYLIGHT LASTS

I heard him spit into the dust
his rough hands rubbing together
then cool mud on my blind eyelids
"Go and wash in the pool of Siloam"

My friend came with me
so I wouldn't stumble
the cool breeze ruffled my hair
as we came over the hill

I knelt at the edge
bent over and splashed water on my face
splash, splash, rubbing my eyes
the silky mud came off
I could feel my eyelashes
light coming through the lids

I opened them a crack
bright sun glints on pool water
I squinted to make out shapes
then turned toward the hill
this glory of golden flowers
the first clear thing I saw.

ROGER NASH

ROGER NASH, born in the London blitz, raised in Egypt and Singapore, came to Canada in 1965. A professor of Philosophy at Laurentian University, Sudbury, he also publishes on ethics and literary criticism.

This plucky performer of poetry has had poems win annual prizes from ARC and Fiddlehead. His latest book, *In the Kosher Chow Mein Restaurant*, won the 1997 Jewish Book Awards' Prize for Poetry.
EMAIL: rnash@nickel.laurentian.ca

A DEFENCE OF PROSE-POETRY

Poetry should abandon parties early to go to a funeral; then try to come back, but get stuck in a phone-booth, reading the lives of all of the names. It should put flowers first on the grave-digger's grave.

Poetry builds roads from a man to a woman, over otherwise impassable terrain. For the very young, or very old, it builds roads rolled up quietly in the heart.

Poetry walks across mine-fields ahead of young children, trying to blow off its own feet first. But it's not afraid, if children laugh and follow, of being accused of leading the way.

Some poems deliberately leave the garden shed unlocked, with an old mattress inside it, beside an excited-to-bursting potato sack.

Poetry checks coats unobtrusively at the Learned Societies, but gets no tips. Afterwards, it empties the pockets of great philosophers and historians, and shares out small change with pan-handlers on the street.

It's a multi-coloured ice-cream that shivers down your throat. Yet it's also the purple mitt frozen to a garbage-truck.

Poetry is that old bag-lady, living in a card-board villa by the railway tracks. She has documents of mercy and papers of peace in the pockets of her unravelling coat. People hurry past, but quite a few take them.

BLUES FOR ALL THE SIMILES: ON READING THE "NATIONAL ENQUIRER"

At the check-out counter, reading the "National Enquirer" is like:

Wanting to become a talkative Trappist monk
Drinking tap-water but getting more and more drunk
Waking on the floor when I'm sure I took top bunk

Even walking down the aisle with a beautiful pregnant nun
Trying to guess whether it's war, or peace, that's just begun
Zipping up my pants but feeling quite undone

      And I'm waitin' for yuh, baby

Seeing signatures on an anarchists' anonymous plot
Dancing a waltz that turns into a Euclidean gavotte
Struggling with a slip-on shoe that won't unknot

Perhaps catching the book-rack at a bus-station picking its nose
Believing defence lawyers who say we didn't do what we chose
Pulling on a Wellington boot that turns into prose

      And I'm still waitin', baby

Noticing the blind man reach for his well polished telescope
- Or the id tying Freud to his couch 'til he's given up hope
Herding cattle onto trucks as men bound with rope

Hearing Mahler's symphonies streaming out of a tap
Struggling with a ticking box that won't unwrap
Breaking down on a road, and in a country, that isn't on the map

      And I'll wait for ever, baby

PROHIBITIONS: GRANDFATHER'S PARTING WORDS OF ADVICE

Never open a dovecote,
and let the sky fill, from ground up, with a flurry of clouds;
stay awake just to keep company with the insomnia of the seas;
marry a girl any taller than a news-stand;
or catch songs in a cage before the bird has flown.

Whatever you do, don't ever
let maiden aunts flicker like candles in a darkened room;
get drunk and buy yourself another sober piano;
set fire to keys of motel rooms where love made you unhappy;
or block your ears to celestial harmonicas in the stars.

Don't, but just don't,
write a poem that turns women into aeroplanes;
speak a completely different language in your dreams;
deny that truth can be found in freshly-baked bread;
or let egg-yolks and justice slip away through your fingers.

Don't fail to distinguish
the sigh let loose by slaughter from the sigh let loose
in love; forget ships tow aromatic islands
laden with camomile, basil, hyssop and bird-shit;
or scorn small feet under a big bed-sheet;

Never, never, ever,
let your eyelids droop with complete serenity,
or with leaden covers of scornful judgement; try to
save yourself; try not to save yourself;
or watch butterflies through a polished brass telescope.

And, whatever you do, try to STOP writing poetry.

THE FORECAST FOR YOUR REGION TOMORROW

Excellent conditions for infidelities on the hills;
but particularly cool in bank-vaults and valleys.
Humility will be low, both in summer and winter.
There will be fog in many friendships and boardrooms.
We shall misplace each other. Still, hems will generally
rise higher than record temperatures.
In first marriages, and last, it won't be moderate.
Even humming-birds are tinder-dry:
no untended angers should be lit.
There will be high waves in daughters' dreams,
and, afterwards, uneasy calms at breakfast-tables.
Sunrise will keep getting earlier in middle-age.
Yet hope will be constantly renewed between somebody's
legs. On washing-lines, bikini bottoms
will flutter overnight, exact and triangular:
a semaphore for both safe and unsafe anchorages.
The radar shows no god
is approaching. They are just clouds with a holy,
purplish light. The only response
to all of our questions is thunder. Is lightning.

A Girl Walks by in a Benediction of Jeans

Whenever she walks by, the traffic lights
all turn to Forgive. And then Go.
Monks in the monastery garden pray
more and more eagerly, counting
every single black bead.
Even some nuns in the convent kitchen
hitch up their habits, and hop
the pink-legged wall. The Devil
himself, selling matches at the corner,
has his eyes completely put out
at his raggedy elbows, staring disconsolately
in two completely different directions:
to worship, or destroy?

When she dabs a bottle of perfume behind her ears,
she re-calibrates the traffic lights again,
according to her mood. Stop, stop.
Stall your life, so long as I'm free.
I'm walking slowly, then fast. I'm not yours.
I'm successfully me. Her red high-heeled
shoes go knock-knock on the side-walk.
The whole street says, immediately,
Come in, come in!

A CREATION STORY

A man walks through a river,
carrying a bicycle above his head,
two sweet potatoes
in his pocket for supper. The river
is brown, foam-backed,
but otherwise unremarkable; the bicycle,
furred with rust; a potato,
weeping with rot, though probably
stolen. Whoever you are,
that man is your father. You wait
to be formed, if he and your mother-to-be
should meet, and can gather their strength.

RAINBOWS

Rabbit flaps lumpily in a snare.
Weasel drifts mist-soft nearer the nest.
The early train from the suburbs draws into the city,
and mannequins in windows wake up from their rest.

There are sewers at the end of some rainbows,
and gold at the beginning of some dreams.
That's why the fiddler in the subway bends his bow,
and passing shopgirls straighten their thoughts and seams.

SEVERAL DIFFICULTIES WITH JUDGING DISTANCES

The tin plate of my childhood clattered
to the floor — like a distant star spinning
with yolk-light and twinkling sugar. Can I lick
the sky clean, before my brother?

In summer rain, secret military
mushrooms fill the field overnight,
sweeping the sky for incoming messages,
prepared for both search and rain to be endless.

The sunrise continually denies it ever
slept with a woman. But women continually
sleep with the sunrise, silk petticoats
rustling and drifting over us every dawn.

Small women usually parachute
furthest, through the home-permed cumulus
of their mounting hair. Once on the ground,
they reassemble quickly, as commandos of love.

A girl's red lips are formed around
the most ancient of languages. She whispers
to me in a forgotten tongue, so I can't quite recall
who said me. It's almost on the tip of who I am.

AFTER THE CATCH

Three fishermen swap chipped
and tea-stained words, sipping
from mugs of loosened teeth. In the dusk,
fish-scales scattered in the grass
stubbornly refuse to give up their light:
a distant galaxy lost among the closing
suns of dandelions; with a pole-star
shining to starboard of the mole-hills,
bright as an unwinking halibut's eye.

Sorted into pails: skate, plaice,
hake and herring. And in the largest and most
dented pail of all, soft
guts, still digesting their own
gelatinous glow. Catch after catch,
on any mackerel's face, there's the same mackerel's
face, that mask never slipping,
giving absolutely nothing away.

By the fishermen's hut, something jumps
from the tall grass into a wicker basket:
shrimps mixed with crickets for supper,
sprinkled with rich red peppers
of fireflies. My father tosses still
twitching shrimps into the boiling pan.
They leap out again, as promptly as strings
of firecrackers, only to fall back in
with antennae as brittle and snapped as a smash
of pansy stalks after a sudden storm.

In mussel shells, thickening tongues
lift, and loll up and down,
already too gummy with air
to get out of their own way;

the words for an incoming tide forever
eluding them. Deep in the bouillabaisse, bones
as fine as cobwebby harps sway
among the bubbling fennel bushes of a Babylon.

Further back in the yard, snails embroider
the incinerator's bricks with a silvery thread,
as whole tides of fish-heads
are turned into a fine soil for sowing
prize-winning dahlias; the ferocity
of saw-toothed waves filed
by flames into soft-tipped pink
petals in the church-hall, under the omniscient
eye of yet another adjudicating vicar.

THE WOMAN OF YOUR DREAMS

I am the woman of your deepest dreams.
I have a way of slipping under your eyelids
as you fall asleep, without even knocking.
I make myself comfortable before you arrive,
and wait for you there, sipping a long purple
cocktail, while dangling my orange heels.
The next morning, you look for me everywhere.
Stopped at a red light, you see me
crossing the road in a crowd. You recognize
the freckles behind my knees, and even my feet,
which left unforgettable prints on the wall
above your bed, resplendent in body-paints.
Tonight, you will dream of getting lost
in my dark and stormy closet, full
of green sandals and black silk
dresses, rustling like an avenue of trees.
When you step out of your car to follow me,
I will turn a corner, and slip elegantly
into yet another face. Sometimes,
as you enter a lingering elevator, you can detect
my empty perfume. But it isn't in any
of the phials shop-assistants can show you,
when you try to buy it for some other woman.

I am the recurring woman of your constant
dreams. You know me better than you know
your wife, your lover, or even Gloria,
your lover's best friend. You know me
better than you once knew your mother.
When we meet at last, in some down-town motel,
and when I lower myself onto you, undulating slowly,
brushing your lips, your nipples, your chest,
your thighs, with the flowing incense of my long
black hair, breasts as quivering

as fish, your back will arch uncontrollably,
like a man on a defibrillator. You will enter my charge
completely and finally. No-one will find
a trace of you the next morning, except
for a sock beneath the bed, in a distinctive tartan
pattern. You'll scream, "I'm drowning!", "I'm drowning!",
against my black-glossed lips. I'll whisper back,
"You're dreaming", "You're dreaming", and a speared octopus
will spurt the room indelibly full of ink.

THE NECESSITY OF QUARRELS
— for Dylan and Caitlin Thomas

United we fall, divided we stand.
Only the weather-cock can referee.
Thunder comes in like a raggedy band.

Can knife-throwers' knives return to the hand?
We find, by knocking, that we've lost a key.
United we fall, divided we stand.

Calm crabs make large tank-tracks over the sand.
When we often fall out, we most agree.
Thunder comes in like a raggedy band.

Moons down a well are almost as grand, but
upside-down lovers smile under the quay.
United we fall, divided we stand.

Can the sea go out, and leave much less land?
We sit on the porch, get drunk on cold tea.
Thunder comes in like a raggedy band.

The more we give in, the more we demand.
Steamed-up windows somehow help us to see.
United we fall, divided we stand.
Thunder comes in like a raggedy band.

TAWATINAW VALLEY FARM

On the hill-side, fields
of rape are hung out to dry,
like urine-stained quilts.

At the spring, deer-prints
gather in the mud, filling
themselves with water.

The farmer walks out
to check his scarecrow. But it's
the scarecrow walks back.

While four horses sleep,
one keeps watch, nudging them with
a mouth-full of thyme.

In the root-cellar,
a lone potato dreams of
bins of harvest moons.

Cows lick morning frost
from each other. Expecting
the sharp taste of salt?

After the first snow,
white saddles appear on each
unbroken black horse.

As snow melts, the road
through the village floods badly
with children in boots.

MESSENGERS

The messengers always shook dust from their feet,
and great distances tumbled from their eyes.
They began to arrive in the very first
town, just the other side of the story.
(Language streamed overhead like clouds.)
They always left more suddenly than they'd come,
stepping back through a thousand and one
unfixed gates of narrative that swung
open for them in the desert air. No-one else
could follow them. When they'd gone, events generally
unfolded as unwisely as before. Even
men's shadows got strung from the trees.
None of the messengers ever returned,
to deepen a friendship. They were condemned, by
      the well-crafted
annals of their lives, never to meet
anyone twice. At best, they might enjoy
a desperately sudden intimacy, before
they were unceremoniously unwritten out of the writhing
sheets into a thin and unpanting air,
still spilling their disappearing seed;
until set down by another story-teller
in a quite different territory, with a new
message to deliver, after yet another
long journey from they could hardly remember where.

With messengers, too, life imitates art
like an irrepressible cockatoo. Our century fills
with uprooted people, perpetually at the end
of another day's journey, eager
to meet anyone twice in the transit
camps. Empty distances stick,
unfalling, in their gummed-up eyes; grease-stained
dust clogs their feet. They carry

messages from whole continents that evicted them.
But now the messages are meant for themselves.
It is their own lives they seek to deliver,
in an endless stream from the smoke on the horizon.
Knock-knock. Am I in enough to listen to myself?

THE UNIVERSITY OF SILENCE

This is the curriculum of the University of Silence.
Students will provide questions for all
of the answers asked.

Why did the Byzantine Empire fail,
its bearded murals glittering wildly,
stigmata showering down golden leaf?
The speed of light remains constant through the universe.

What can prove the existence of God?
A small cloud that beats a loud tambourine.
Alternatively, but as successfully, a Smyrna fig.

Why do long-lasting marriages fail?
Yellow umbrellas may open more slowly than blue.

What, then, is love?
Two snails climb a cabbage stump.
They don't turn back. Tracks shine.

Was Socrates a Philosopher, or a husband who could think?
Red umbrellas fold as slowly as blue.

Why are there wars, still?
The speed of snails is constant through the universe.

Now unwrite your name, and lose this paper.

WEDDING IN THE GARDEN

Is the bride ready?
She smooths her gown. Snails still have
one horn out, one in.

Ancestors are here.
Well under the deck, inchworms
measure joists carefully.

Ready? The groom picks
white cat hairs from his jacket.
So the mice won't know?

Husk of a beetle.
It must've jumped the gun, and
eloped already.

Flowers wave and peer
at people sown carefully
in neat rows of chairs.

Crickets in the hedge
start their solemn service first.
Like us, some can't sing.

A clump of rhubarb
frames the Rockies. One bug climbs
several peaks at once.

The best man sweats in
formal dress. Snails under
trees strip to the waist.

Dry summer wedding.
The heron's one long leg grows
longer, grows longer.

A huge frog and the
groom's father exchange glances.
The man hops away.

A lily turns blue,
instantly. Will the bridesmaid
smile? Pigeon droppings.

As rings are exchanged,
a truck rumbles by. Even
bird-tables tremble.

A bee slurps into
a daisy. Drunk already,
before the champagne.

The watching mountains
swallow clouds in blessing, and
hold up blue brocade.

A dragonfly lands
on a tall wobbly radish.
Balance! It's easy.

Even flea bites are
enjoyable, when they're felt
at a son's wedding.

The bride's eyes are as
bright and blue as pools well-stocked
with hard-to-catch fish.

We raise our glasses.
Bubbles make us sneeze. All the
grasshoppers jump once.

SONJA DUNN

SONJA DUNN, Toronto creator of 10 children's books of rhythm, rhyme, rap, chant & song, and poet in many adult anthologies, is an all round kick starter. She travels the world with her guitar, story-skirt and hat, performing her work.

Her 30 year long run TV show "Sonja Dunn and Company" for CBC, CTV and Rogers Cable Systems promotes Canadian culture. Described as "a high octane conglomerate and an off-the-wall dynamo", her books include *Butterscotch Dreams, Primary Rhymerry, Crackers and Crumbs, Rapunzul's Rap, Beauty and the Beast Rap, Gimme a Break, Rattlesnake* and *Keeping Fit.*

LETTER

Dear Ms Finch,
this morning
I found one of your
tiny naked babies
on my balcony
right under
the iron sculpture
where you have
built your nest
for the last three years.
The fledgling must have fallen out
because I saw you
flying to and fro frantically,
your rose-breasted mate
on the wing
beside you.

It was at the very moment
that I read in the morning paper
about the crack-head
who had murdered her
own helpless child.

When I opened the sliding door
you flew away.
I was only going to put
the little one
back in the nest.

Come back,
have a good breakfast.

IN UKRAINE

In Ukraine's Vorzel Forest
the dampness of my dacha

seeps into my bones
through the thick slab
of a too short mattress
which assaults my pampered body.

How many tee-shirts
does it take
to keep warm?

That ancient Ukrainian moon
transparent like vodka
forces her way
through bars
of unscreened windows
and lays her head
on my pillow.

She tells me,
"Nothing is easy in Ukraine."

CANADA TAVERN

She was young once
long ago
slimmer and softer smiling,
had some grand future
manicuring
hairdressing
maybe dancing
at Arthur Murray's,
light on her size sixes.

Flimsy red sheer blouse
swinging taffeta skirt
a flower in her fluffy feather cut.
Evening in Paris,
Tweed by Yardley,
scent of sweet warm breath
through straight little teeth.

Now
rockin' and rollin' unsteadily
on worn out Hush Puppies
dirty white scarf
fat from too many drafts,
she is hard
like a ball and chain

NORTH COUNTRY

This North country's too hard for me.
Nothing melts it
not even an August sun.

I stay in black slag caverns,
stalactites stretch icy fingers
touching and freezing
my tight white ass.

This north
a creosote coffin
envelopes my life
and holds fast.

MY D.P.'S

They came off the boat
fat from potatoes
weary and confused.

At thirteen
the embarrassment
from all the wet
tearfilled kisses
caused me to shrink
behind a pillar.

MEMORIES OF WOLODYMYR SEROTIUK'S BIRTHDAY

Sometimes, riding on a train
I think of you in the thirties
and can hardly keep from crying.

We were a carousel
governed by an out of whack calliope
gypsying
from Toronto to Geraldton
to Fort Francis
to Timmins
to Kenora
to Port Arthur-Fort William
to Sudbury
to Coniston
to Rouyn, Noranda
then back to Toronto.

Always back to Toronto
where we had to leave the baby Mama had.

Standing six four
a stately hussar
wearing spats, watch chain and fedora
you held my skinny six-year-old hand.
We were a pair
riding the rails.

Mama died in thirty seven
left me with you.
"Poison in the born parts," you told me.
The Catholic Children's Aid
said a man couldn't look after a little girl
properly
but we fooled them

didn't we
and ran away away together.

They got Ronnie though.
He was only two days old.
"Some good family
will adopt the baby," Miss Jeffrey pronounced.

"Vee Ukrainians
no let people adopt our babies.
Vee no sign avay cheeldren," you said.

And we never did.

VEECHNAYA PAMYAT
(Eternal Memory)

Too young at five
to know
my mother's eyes
were forever shuttered.

Long pine coffin
in the hollow room
a vague memory now,
picked up
by six strong men
and carried across
the highway
to St. Theresa's church.

No hearse
no cars
only a poor procession
Ukrainian immigrants
chanting
"Veechnaya Pamyat"
the eternal memory dirge.

THE GIFT

Amid simmering samovars
the sombre colours
of the designer scarf
you gave me
that were not
in my fashion palette
fit in so well.

Those Ukrainian flowers
purple asters
and marigolds
were reminiscent
of our garden walks.

You never made it
to Ukraine
but your echoing voice
was in the beehives
and windmills

BABYN YAR

Babyn Yar
Babyn Yar
Babyn Yar
to celebrate the slaughter
the drums beat
the tanks roar
the aircraft circle
to mask deafening reports
from Nazi soldiers' guns
"We are drunk
we stagger
we are wild
we become inhuman
we cannot hear
we cannot really see
these unclothed bodies
of the maimed
of the women
of the children
of gypsies Jews Ukrainians
falling
falling
falling
into Babyn Yar"

A Canadian writer
I stand on Babyn Yar

It is said that beneath us
we can find brains
babies' shoes
embroidered nannies' blouses
under us lie
the ravaged

Nakedness made them invisible

SINGING SAND

We are the dunes
of singing sand
singing
singing
singing

crystal songs
songs sung low
songs of caravans
songs of camel bells

We are the dunes
singing sand
singing
singing
singing
songs of quartz on wings of wind

songs of mystery
singing
singing
singing
our desert song

SKY KU

Skywriter's white streaks
etch fine lines on azure
writing, "P. S. I love you."

HAIKU

Pelicans at sea
giant cups with wings
fish peak out each side.

MIGRATION

All winter
Canadian snowbirds
are perched
on dialysis machines
in Florida.

BEFORE GLASNOST, OY TOVARISH
(Before Glasnost, Hey Friend)

The Ukrainians
are singing tonight
in the basement
of St. Vladymir's
it's the same old song
the constant one
that they sing
about Ukraine
not dead yet
and they sing about
her glory and freedom
and they sing about
her brothers and sisters
always loyal
and they sing
about the future
not in any poetic phrases
just plain talk
about how Ukraine's foes
will be vanquished
under this new Glasnost.

Oy tovarish,
do you believe
what the Ukrainians
are singing
tonight?

SINGING FOR DINNER

Kyiv bandura busker
strumming outside
St. Sophia's Cathedral
for American dollars
extended arm
caressing his ticket
to dinner
what a saga
his thin fingers pluck:

"Please give me new bills only.
Money changers won't take
anything old."

ADVICE TO A CANADIAN IN PARADISE

"Hey, that's no way
to eat a mango.
Come, come into the warm sea.
Ah, let the sweet
juice drip on your chin
run down
your elbows
to your knees.

Come come,
eat the soft mango.
Now take a swim."

ROBERT SWARD

ROBERT SWARD, winner of a Guggenheim Fellowship, is the author of 16 books, including *A Much-Married Man* and *Four Incarnations, New & Selected Poems*. Winner of WebScout's Way Cool Site Award for editing eSCENE 1996, Sward has contributed to over 200 literary journals and e-Zines.

Having lived in many North American places (cities to island retreats), now he serves as contributing editor for several publications and teaches for the University of California Extension in Santa Cruz. EMAIL: sward@cruzio.com
Website: http://www.cruzio.com/~scva/rsward.html

SCARLET THE PARROT
Saanichton, B.C.

Scarlet perches on the office windowsill
shrieking, hollering, barking

Like a dog. She knocks her mottled beak
against the warehouse window

And tries to open
the metal hook and eye latch.

There are parrot droppings
on the telephone and Scarlet has eaten

Part of the plastic receiver.
The parrot slides like a red fireman

With yellow and blue feathers
up and down the cord,
            holding on

With her beak, maneuvering gracefully
            with her claws.
When I approach she calls, "Hello, hello…"

Walks up my trouser leg holding on
with her macaw's beak. I feed the bird

Oranges and pears, almonds
and sunflower seeds.

I swivel my head round and round
in imitation of her neck movements.

"What's happening?" she asks,
and again, "What's happening?"

"Hello, cookie. Yoo-hoo...
Can you talk, can you talk?" she asks

Chewing for several minutes,
finally swallowing
            a leather button

Off my green corduroy jacket, threatening,
ready to tear my ear off,

Biting if I place my finger
in her mouth. Her tongue is black

And her beady eyes piercing like an eagle's.
She wants a response, tests my reactions.

Tenderly the parrot walks up my corduroy jacket,
sensually restraining her claws. I'm aroused.

When a dog barks, she barks too: Rrf, rrf.
Casually, a relaxed but authentic

Imitation. "Hello, darling," she breathes,
looking me in the eye knowing I know

If it pleases her she might bite my ear off.
"Yoo-hoo, yoo-hoo, now you say something," she says.

THE BIGGEST PARTY ANIMAL OF THEM ALL

Spoke Hindi, a little English,
suffered from diabetes,
   was allergic to incense,
flowers and perfume,

loved chocolate,
       gave it away, used it as prasad,
a gift to his disciples.

In his 70s he gave himself away,
reportedly 'poking' as many as 300
of his youngest followers.

'Now's your chance,' he'd say, his mouth full.
'That's right, that's right. Lie back,
meditate,' he'd croon. 'Have faith.'

The dude separated so many people from so much money
he had to create the Guru Om Foundation.
Rolls Royces, chauffeurs, ashrams in all the major cities.

The movement started small, twenty,
     thirty,
         then hundreds,
           soon —

     doctors, lawyers,
hoteliers, cocaine dealers and professors,
       dancers, artists
and musicians

     flocked to him,
himself a musician, masked actor, comic,
   storyteller
       extraordinaire.

Flatulent, potbellied old mystic,
giver-away of toys, party hats and favours to devo-
tees.
The 'hundred-hatted yogi' we called him.

God, he was fun to be around!

Festivals with world-renowned performers,
dinner for five thousand,
                              and, afterwards,
we got to approach and touch his feet.

True, sometimes he'd flip out, become enraged,
have to be strapped down
or held,
          one devotee at each limb.
'Kill.' 'Fuck.' 'Destroy,' he'd holler,
Rudra the Howler.

Then, reviving,
'Chant.' 'Dance.' 'Meditate.'
Nataraj, the dancing Shiva, O graceful one!

Once, mid-revelry, enraged at something I'd written,
he drew back, swatted me four, five times
with a mass of peacock feathers. Whoosh! Whoosh!
Whoosh!

It's known as Shaktipat, kick-start Kundalini yoga,
where the party thrower has only to touch someone
—
blow to the head or soft caress —

and Zap! that person awakens.

For two, maybe three, minutes
I saw two worlds, one
interpenetrating the other

silver suns, pin points
      of electric whiteness
jewels interpenetrating jewels.

World 'A' and world 'B'
as one vibrating blue pearl,
expanded inhabitable consciousness

world without end
world like a skyful of blue suns
Whoosh! Whoosh! Whoosh!

Head spinning, I began to laugh,
and he too, old cobra face,
      began to howl,
mister three in one. Mister one in three.

O thou paunchy one
      in Birkenstocks
            and orange silk robe, trickster,
magician,
      master cocksman,
hit me again!

Seven years I hung out with him,
even flew to India, meditated
            in his cave
chanting to
      scorpions, malaria-bearing mosquitoes
so illumined they chanted back.

          phallic god,

god in the shape of a dick,
    godfather
    con man

god of wind,
    lord of animals,
killer god, god of death
and destroyer of all life
    one in three,
    three in one.

'Sonofabitch,' I say
'Sonofabitch!'
The guests are still arriving,
the party's just begun.

TURNING 60

*"The first 40 years of life give us the text; the next 30
supply the commentary on it."*
— Schopenhauer

1. HOMEWORK

According to Webster, the word **six** derives from the
Latin
"sex" [s-e-x] and the Greek "hex" [h-e-x].
Six units or members
as, an ice-hockey team;
a 6-cylinder engine;
sixfold, six-pack, sixpenny nail, six-
shooter, sixth sense.

"Zero" denotes the absence of all magnitude, the
point of departure
in reckoning; the point from which the graduation of
a scale
(as of a thermometer) begins;
zero hour,
zeroth,
as, "the zero power of a number."

Zero, the great "there's nothing there" number,
a blast off into a new decade.

2. GRAMMAR AS HYMNAL

Seeking solace in a review of grammar,
I turned to Strunk & White's
Elements of Style. Standing at attention,
opening to the section on usage, I chanted and sang —
uniting my voice with the voices of others, the vast

chorus
of the lovers of English.

We sing of verb tense, past, present and future.
We sing the harmony of simple tenses.
We lift our voice in praise of action words,
and the function of verb tense.

We sing of grammar which is our compass
providing, as it does, clues as to how
we might navigate the future,
at the same time it
illuminates the past.

As a teacher, **I talk**. That's present.
For 30 years as a teacher, **I talked**. That's past.
It may only be part time, but **I will talk**. That's future.

3. LIVING THE FUTURE PERFECT

I will have invoked the muse.

I will have remembered to give thanks, knowing our origins
are in the invisible, and that we once possessed boundless
energy,
but were formless, and that we are here to know 'the
things of the heart
through touching.'

I will have remembered, too, that there is only one thing
we all possess equally and that is our loneliness.

I will have loved.
You will have loved.
We will have loved.

ON MY WAY TO THE KOREAN WAR...
— for President Dwight Eisenhower

On my way to the Korean war,
I never got there.
One summer afternoon in 1952,
I stood instead in the bow
of the Attack Transport Menard,
with an invading force
of 2,000 battle-ready Marines,
watching the sun go down.
Whales and porpoises,
flying fish and things jumping
out of the water.
Phosphoresence —
Honolulu behind us,
Inchon, Korea, and the war ahead.

Crewcut, 18-year-old librarian,
Yeoman 3rd Class, editor
of the ship's newspaper,
I wrote critically if unoriginally
of our Commander-in-Chief,
Mr. President,
and how perplexing it was that he
would launch a nuclear-powered submarine
while invoking the Lord,
Crocodile Earthshaker,
Shiva J. Thunderclap,
choosing the occasion to sing
the now famous Song of the Armaments,
the one with the line "weapons for peace":

O weapons for peace,
O weapons for peace,

> awh want, awh want
> more weapons for peace!

At sundown, a half dozen sailors
converged on the bow of the ship
where, composed and silent,
we'd maintain our vigil
until the sun had set.

Careful to avoid being conspicuous,
no flapping or flailing of the arms,
no running, horizontal take-offs,
one man, then another, stepped out into space,
headed across the water,
moving along as if on threads.
After a while, I did the same:
left my body just as they left theirs.

> In-breathe, out-breathe, and leave,
> in-breathe, out-breathe, and leave.
> Leave your body, leave your body,
> leave your body, leave your body,

we sang as we went out
to where the light went,
and whatever held us to that ship
and its 2,000 battle-ready troops, let go.
So it was, dear friends, I learned to fly.
And so in time must you
and so will the warships,
and the earth itself,
and the sky,
for as the prophet says, the day cometh
when there will be no earth left to leave.

> O me, O my,
> O me, O my,
> goodbye earth, goodbye sky.
> Goodbye, goodbye.

42 POETS NAMED ROBERT

1.

Yes, I met Robert Frost and Robert Lowell and Robert Creeley, and Robert
Duncan and Robert Mezey, Robert Bly and Robert Peterson, appeared in *A
Controversy of Poets, An Anthology of Contemporary American Poetry* edited
by Robert Kelly, but not in *New Poets of England and America* edited by
Robert Pack, admire the work of Robert Bridges, Robert Browning, Robert
Burns, Bobbie Creeley, Robert Dana, Robert Finch, Roberto Galvan, Robert
Graves, Robert Hass, Robert Herrick, Robert Hogg, Yo! Bob Holman, Robert
Huff, Robert Kroetsch, Robert Lax, Robbie McCauley, Robert McGovern,
Roberta Mandel, Robert Peters, Robert Pinsky, Robert Southey, Robert Louis
Stevenson and Roberto Vargas, and even performed in taverns and coffee
houses in London, Ontario, and in Toronto at Major Robert's
Restaurant — near the intersection of Major and Robert Streets — with Canadian
poets Robert Priest and Robert Zend, the three of us, billed as the Three
Roberts, dedicating our readings to CBC Radio's Robert Weaver and Robert
Prowse, to the literary critic Robert Fulford, with half a dedication to my
friend John Robert Colombo, and to Robert Service.

2.

But as each of my four wives explained, patiently or otherwise, over a
period of three decades, "Robert, it doesn't pay. Robert, there's no
future in it. I'm not going to go on like this…" and "Robert, doesn't
it depress you to go into libraries and see all those poetry books by all
those other writers named Robert, even the ones not named Robert, that
practically no one on earth is going to read?" "Well, yes, it's true it
doesn't pay. And it's true there's no future in it. And it does depress
me that practically no one in America reads poetry, and that is why I took
a job writing software user manuals after teaching for fourteen years. But then
unable to let go of what I'd done, resigned in order to go back and
write some more poetry. And today I think of you all as I re-read this
morning's mail."

"Three letters. One from Robert Priest, the Canadian poet. He writes of
the death by drowning of the poet Robert Billings, and the deaths also of
poets not named Robert. And Earle "Robert" Birney, he says, who, at 75 was
seen by the editor of *New: American & Canadian Poetry* in a Toronto
rainstorm in the throes of love running up Yonge Street bearing flowers
for his 35-year-old sweetheart; Birney who, at 79 fell out of a tree from
which he'd been trying to dislodge a kite, and who, not long after,
recovering from an injured hip, resumed cycling on a regular basis at
breakneck speed through a North Toronto cemetery; Birney, he says, alive
and in his 80s, has visitors who read him his poems, poems that, when
Birney hears them, with impaired memory, he enjoys, though he is
unable to understand he is the author of those poems."

"Letter #2: Nicky 'Bob' Drumbolis, proprietor of a Toronto bookstore,
writes that his rent has gone up $700 a month, that he must give up the
store, and that he is "earnestly clearing stock for the big move.""

"And Roberto 'Robbie' Roberts, publisher of my last book, writes that he
has become part owner of Omega Apparel, a business to which he now devotes
all his time. He's not doing any more poetry these days, only neckties."

3.

I drift off at my computer and dream of Robert Zend, whose heart gave out
four years ago, and of Robert Priest and Robert Graves, and in the dream I
see myself reading my favourite Graves poems to Graves, and he is lucid as
my father before his heart stopped at 82, and just before I wake, Graves
tells me I am a cross between Halley's comet and Rip Van Winkle the way I
go off to England, France, Mexico, Canada, and then, years later, return,
meeting the sons and daughters of the people, of the Roberts, for example,
I once knew, and that is what poems are supposed to do, and that I
have been living more like a poem than a man with his feet on the ground,
and that in the time that remains I should be living more like a man with
his feet on the ground and less like a poem.

SEX & TV WITH AUNT MIRIAM — 1945

"Always wash your hands after you've played in the backyard with those leaves and things before touching yourself," said my aunt, beginning our affair with this public service announcement.

"Yes, m'am."
"Eddie, I'm going to show you how broadminded I am."
"Okay."
"But first I want you to tell me what you do with Lenore and her sister."
"Nuthin."
"You spin the bottle?"
"Yeah."

Luminous brown-eyed Miriam abuzz with heat,
My left arm around her, my right hand
in her right hand
         "Kiss me   love me   feel me, Eddie..."

I'm a pleaser. But... what was it she wanted me to do?

                          A seventh grader, I'd been held
back a year at school. "He tries hard, and he's smart about some things,
but..." Anyway, I was right in there for a while with the slow
learners.

Four thousand feet down in a North of England coal mine,
I'd just have grabbed a shovel and gotten to work.
I'd have known right away what to do.

Holding me with one hand,
marking with the other,
D-I-C-K, wrote my twenty-something aunt.
Hmm. It felt good.

She finished by drawing some arrows and a bull's eye on her own body.

What was it like? It was like television, "informative and entertaining."
Never to have been fucked and never to have watched television either,
and then to be fucking and watching the evening news
on one of the first TVs in Chicago, and the Atomic
Bomb going off and the war over all at the same time, I think...
the truth is, I still don't understand.

The diagrams and the lettering helped.
I like seeing things labelled.
I'm so grateful.

"All art aspires to the state of music." That's true. I know that. And
even at thirteen I loved Gershwin ("Rhapsody in Blue"), but I knew real
music when I heard it. "O do me, thrill me." And *that's* what I went for.
That's what I learned at thirteen. And *that's* what I'm grateful for.

O Miriam, say it again. Tell me where you want it. Draw me a
picture.
Ah, dearest, how helpful it's been having those letters printed on
my dick.

How many times have I been told,
"Eddie, you don't know your ass from a hole in the ground"?
More times
than there are stars in the sky. And I hold my head high. At least I know
where, O Aunt Miriam, O Miriam, to look for my dick.

PORTRAIT OF AN L.A. DAUGTHER

Take #1

Braided blonde hair
white and pink barrettes
Bette Davis gorgeous
I hug her
dreamy daughter with no make-up
silver skull and crossbones
middle ("don't mess with me")
          finger
                    ring
three or four others in each ear
rings in her navel
rings on her thumbs
gentle moonchild
          "pal" she announces
to "Porno for Pyros"
formerly the group "Jane's Addiction"
 "Nothing's Shocking"
with Perry Farrell
Dave Navarro on guitar
and Stephen Perkins
on drums
"Ain't No Right" they sing
she plays it for me loud
"Been Caught Stealing"
          they sing
and "Ted Just Admit It"
"Every body everybody everybody's —"

I hug her
Shalimar fruit smell
Oil of Olay
Wet 'n' Wild lip gloss

diamond stud earrings
and glitter on her cheeks

Hannah Davi — a new name —
walk-on in the movie "Day Of Atonement"
      with Christopher Walken

Wan, she's looking wan
my dancing girl daughter

And a part in a Levitz Furniture ad
      ("it's work")
and a part in an MCI commercial
      ("Best Friends")
breaking in
"Brotherhood Of Justice"
"Lost Boys"
"Private Lessons"

a Swiss Alps bar-maid
("classic blonde Gretel")
in a Folger's Coffee commercial

"Grunge is in" she says
visiting Santa Cruz
"any Goodwill's around?"

   *   *   *

Flashback

Appearing,
      "crowning" says the doctor

"Hannah" says her mother
"the name means 'grace'"

Two-year-old drooling
as lying on my back
I toss her into space
and back
      she falls
and back
into space again

Flawless teeth and perfect smile
one blue eye slightly larger than the other
her three thousand miles away mother
still present as
two as one
two breathing together
we three breathe again as one
Hannah O Hannah

"HOT SUGAR CHILI SEX"

He's musician
        prophet
a raging Apollo

L.A. Looks   Megahold
        hair gel
gold hoops,
        diamond stud earrings

Toenails and fingernails
        painted black

6'3", 200 pounds
legs propped up
on a wobbly stool

                        Listening
Magic-Red-Blood-Hot-Sugar
        Chili-Sex

"What I see is insanity.
Whatever happened to humanity?"

"Good lyrics," I say

"The Chili Peppers," he says
"it's rap and it sucks.
Actually, I like Punk more —"

White steel guitar in hand
he demonstrates:

"Fuck you..." he sings.
End of demonstration.

Now he's Anthony Keidis
wearing a tube sock

on his dick
"Suck my kiss", he sings

Next he's trancey, anguished
Mr. Sonic Youth

At home:

Washing windows
            falling into grace

scrubbing floors
            dancing
doing
            standup
                  "impressions"

My son the genie
my son Mr. Kleen

Tries to jump into my arms
where do kids come from anyway?

                  "Fucking life
                  Everything sucks," he says

Mourning Kurt Cobain,
            Hillel Slovak and the others
dead of an overdose.

Youthanasia

Whip-smart

Funk Da World
Funk Da World

I'm the father, I'm supposed to tell him—what?

"I know the truth," he says
"I know the truth."

"It's a Gun"

Sara's got on earphones.
I make out Mariah Carey
singing *I want you,*
    I need you,
        don't leave me

Class begins.
"Okay, Sara," I say,
"tune her out."
Never be alone at night,
if you're lonely, love will be there, Carey sings.

Student turns it up loud, then takes off the phones.

Marco, New Yorker,
walks in late,
begins yelling from his seat
at some guy at the door
who's shaking his fist,

but Marco isn't leaving,
he's staying put, and his friend,
clearly pissed, won't let up. *Mutha...*
waves and yells he's been robbed,
wants his money back,

Yeah, right. Yeah, yeah. Uh huh
What are we on about today? I've got this
lesson plan. I mark the guy late.
"Cool it, Marco, you're late again," I say.
I still don't know he's got a gun

"Let's talk about this outside,"
and the other kid disappears
and Marco steps outside
and I tell him to go home.
Actually, he's written this B+ essay

about "murder and bang bang"
how home was a front stoop in Manhattan,
how he's here for his safety,
how he can't get used to "San-ty Cruz"
he misses all that bad company.

"Teach," he says, "I'm not goin' home."

I'm pissed and he's telling me to cool it.
"You don't know what I got," he's saying.
He's right. I don't know. Then the police
are all around us; turns out
the room's barricaded. How did I know

Murder and bang bang. Mariah Carey singing
It's a gun, it's a gun.

JAMES REANEY

JAMES REANEY was born in 1926 on a farm in South Easthope near Stratford, Ontario. One room school (Rime of the Ancient Mariner); collegiate (Wuthering Heights, Paradise Lost, Homer); scholarships to University College, Toronto (Beowulf, Edith Sitwell, Anglo Saxon Street); terrorized campus with a short story, "The Box Social" and a poem about abortion; first job: Creative Writing or Writhing at Manitoba University; married the poet, Colleen Thibaudeau, two children at present in publishing; doctorate with Northrop Frye — "Vala or the Four Zoas"!

He has *Performance Poems* recently as well as *Box Social & Other Stories*. He's crazy about the Donnellys: topic of 3 plays. His over 30 titles include books for young and old, plays and 3 co-authored operas. This winner of three Governor General Awards (2 - poetry, 1 - drama) is now a retired professor from Western University, London, Ontario.

THE SHIP

Out of trees was I made, Oak & Elm.
Up in Canada strong men were sent
To search for, cut down & trim
A four century pine for my mast,
For the unbreakable bow
Of my white wings' electric
Energy-string.
At first when they launched me,
From the cold & salt water I shied
Still thinking & dreaming
Rain water forest thoughts,
But soon live could I not
Without
The sea's wet.
At first, cross with the currents & tides
Pulling me, pushing me
That lifted me this way & that,
With your help
I learnt to give in to their love.
All the trees in me became
One tree
Who belonged to the sea.
So well had they sawed me, planed me, curved me,
They who for centuries had reckoned the gives
The gives & the takes
Between wood, winter, water
Between artefact and waterflow,
Starsay and air-go.

To contest with another such was I bred,
Carved she was in foreign place south of us.
By no means lacking in gold, her builders.
You were chosen my master.
I, swan-winged with fish-arrow body, I

Obeyed of touches your lightest.
We grew to be one
And race after race we won.

Once at Ile-aux-Sables, the graveyard of many
Dunked sailors, sunk ships,
Trapped one whole night
In a sandy cross-currented inlet,
We fought entrapment & embayment,
An uncomfortable tangle of purposelessnesses

Which at dawn, by a whisker us freeing,
Having sent your crew below deck,
You solved.
So complete was our love for each other,
One mind, one heart, one corps,
Your sail-thoughts I was and your heart-rig
Your man-rudder.

At length, I grew old. Heartless the men
Who dismissed you, knotted my sails
With an engine infested me.
To Hispaniola I carried dried fish,
Fetched back rum & brown sugar,
Fish south, rum north, back, forth,
Year after year,
Until the place to the south
Thinking to defeat us at last
Us again challenged with a boat new
Trimmed with brass, mahogany polished,
Newly wed, strong, young.
Through rough loveless usage, I'd grown
Derelict, cracked, rheumatic,
Shabby & old.

Still, scorning her varnish & modern,
With my sails I hissed at my rival,
For once more I felt your step & touch.
Once more beneath your thigh I rode
So that all through me flew a lightning,
A jump fluid forward us driving,
For you alone recklessly sailing
Swifter & faster than
Any winged ship ever had sailed.
By seamiles we won at the finish line.
As my breaking & splintering then
Came too late to rob us of win.

Never saw you again.
Mast felled, sails sold, put-put
Engine rattling my bones,
With a load of used cars & trucks
Off Haiti I sank
Down to the shark's consolations & coral.

When at the harbour whose yards were my mother
They woke you and told you this news
Of my death while you slept,
I hear, I know that you broke down
And that, you, publicly, wept.

A Novelette Called: Not Proven

Madeleine, quiet, passionate, beautiful,
Daughter of Victorian Glasgow merchant,
Mr. Smith,
Slept, with her kid sister, in a gaslit
Basement bedroom
Next to the kitchen, the water cellar,
With a view of area street railings
And a private entrance from there.
Infatuated was she with Emile L'Angelier
Handsome French dandy, no morals and poor.
At night when clouds raced across the moon
Behind the chimneys and garrets, they met
Secretly in the gaslit basement room.
She was terrified of her father but Emile
Kept insisting that she should tell him
About them. Or he would.
After coming home from the Smith's house,
Where he had drunk cocoa made by Madeleine,
His landlady found him dead.
But Madeleine's lawyer saw to it that never
Did she be called to the witness box,
Got her off!
Later on, the theory arose that Emile,
Knowing that she had bought some arsenic
To put in her hairwash (cf. the plot of Lady Magdalen
Hall's *Airing in a Closed Carriage*)
Himself purchased arsenic and poisoned himself.
Is that why a shrewd Glasgow jury brought in
A verdict of "Not Proven"?

MOSES

Was a young stutterer
Filled with vision-fire
He found so hard
Clearly to utter.
He was
A Cumulus
Cloud 10 miles high
Crushed into a short
Shepherd
Hiding out in the desert
Staring at a bush.
The Bush
Began to burn and crack to him,
Till it smoked in his tongue
Such words of power
He humbled Leviathan
Who opened his jaws
For the exodus
Of this stuttering young man's people.
With pillar of fire
Will pillar of cloud
Burning and unburning
(The Bush again)
Led by this stammerer
They starved in the desert,
But he found them bread.
When they thirsted
Water out of a rock
He knocked
With his rod.
They were unlettered.
From Sinai he brought them
Alphabet.

And at
The last, he led them
To a garden to enter which
He alone was forbidden.
Staring at it
From the desert side of a river
He, a cumulus
Cloud 10 miles high
Compressed into a shepherd,
He looked and he died.

THE CONGRESS CAFÉ

At the Congress Cafe in Austin, Texas,
(We were down there looking at Emily's Mss)
A group of men and women came in,
Having worked all day in some state office.
Along with some snacks, they ordered drinks.

After about twenty minutes
You could have heard what they'd drunk
Happily sudden speak out through them,
And this sound of community went on until we left,
We left for Mrs. William's Hotel
Where all the researchers stay.
I have no doubt that the drink they had taken
Coupled some of them, also, in matching ecstasies
On Murphy beds.

How many things seek out their voice in us?
Unsuspected demons and angels
Wait years for the arrangement we provide
Of gut, enzyme, funny bone, nervous system, mind.

Is it blood, seeking to recirculate once more?
Blood that we lost at Frederick's great battle
When first he conquered Angria?

So did the apples that Elmer Sheerer's father planted
In his orchard by the blue tin house at the tracks.
Young Elmer grew up to press these into cider barrels
Whose liquor he drank and played wild, harmonica music
Poured from a Pippin tap or a Sugar spigot.
Or did the cider not also pour from a husband
On wilder bed springs,
Printing press of his sons, Stanley and Geordie
Early friends of mine
O Congress café

BRUSH STROKES IN DECORATING A FAN

(a)
In bed at night
I think of you
Downstairs there
In the dark —
Chair, table, cubpoard,
Dishes, books, my outside boots,
Dear good things
That wait
Patient —
Ly
All night
For me and the morning.
Still there
When I get up
And come down
To you.

(b)
A sentence of persons drifts by on Huron Street now
Which started before dawn, ends only at old moon set
With a single last traveller
After midnight long.

(c)
O cloud unreachable in air
O icicle in my gloved hand
O water in your cupped hand.

(d)
This is a blue study:
I see a blue sky above firs blurred with white
Swipes,
We're all in a big, I think,
Bottle round of pale blue ink.

(e)

A jug & basin,
Ewer on the wash stand
Beside my bed at the farm.
Whistling for every crossing
Comes the one o'clock train.
Seven minutes later
The jug shakes…

(f)

Some think they stripped me.
I say, I threw off stale decency
The better to grip the slippery dragon
Whom I pinned with five nails —
Forever!
I have it that
Upright I fought, spouting christening streams,
Rested, relaxed, shrank, down — rose again
Forever!

(g)

Ernie's Barber Salon Near the College.
Mr. Delilah, the barber,
Cuts a field of hair
In his basement shop
When I duck down to see him
In the fraternity field
Scything away.

(h)

Leaves speak all summer ss ss ss ss
""""""""""fall ch ch ch ch ch ch
""""""""""""""winter
""""""""""""""""spring .. ..

(i)
H_2O
My cousin says an element we breathe a lot
Long ago
Also
Married a husband who changes her
to slippery indescribable drinkable uncatchable...

(j)
O dear little babes, crawl quickly away
The Butter Box field in Nova Scotia is after you!

(k)
You dirty "thou" rustler
You've stolen my sex,
Purloined my figurative, miraculous
Jesus.

(l)
Dark of the Moon
Where are you in the Heavens
This dark starry night?
Shall I find you by missing some stars
Blotted out by the veiled face of a nun
Dimly traced out by earthlight?
When at tomorrow's eventide I see your bright sickle,
Shall I still wonder who the night before
Smuggled you unseen across the sky?

(m)
Nubia
Where, twice written language disappeared
And twice human sacrifice returned.

(n)
North of Timmins
Canoeing down the Mattagami
I meet you,
Yellow straw hair,
Mud brown eyes.

(o)
Because I was pretty
You with Medusa
Camera
Changed me into glamorous stone;
Your Belial Ad agency
Changed my name to Rita Hayworth.
You went to bed with her.
You woke up with "me".

(p)
Orchard
First a haw
Small, red, round
next a sour
Red & yellow crab.
Then the Ben Davis,
Scarlet, not ripe until March,
But still even then,
A hog choker
Which you married to Mr. McIntosh
Who smoothed me to the delicious Courtland.

(q)
A curse on the "she" who walked yth
My Larousse Encyclopedia of Myth
From my office.

(r)
This is the wee the farmers for out & pic up stones.
Yes, but what have you left out the "k's"?
The k's are the stones.

(s)
In a chapter of the Bell
I met that learned enharmonic novel —
Ist
Ding Dong!

(t)
You tore my Jesus from his lake
But put no nymph back,
Only a scum
Petroleum.

(u)
A Useful List;
Hermes
Hera
Apollo
Zeus
Venus
Vulcan
Mars
Athena
Vesta
Hades
Poseidon
Ceres.
Useful for what?
Well, I don't quite know yet,
But I swear that as an infant,
Born near the Little Lakes,
I met them.
Every morning in our house,
Vesta used to light the stoves.

(v)
The hand of my ear
Picks up a distant bell.

(w)
I know a book that opens up people
And reads them,
Spreads them out, pleat by pleat,
Till they see as far up as up.
Till they see further than down.
It makes their eyes so sharp
That East or West
They can spot Nobody coming up the Road.

(x)
I know an experience
That brings my 2 butterfly wings
Tight together
Then open
Now shut
Dull blur
Sudden bright.
Over the years our selves
Have been blended
By all this together ...
Pleated and unpleating,
Opening and closing,
Tight together,
Loose apart —
The two sides of a breath.

(y)
Sick, I came to my sister's abbey for refuge
My outlaw forest outside her ruled windows.
In white, she now stands over me
Drinking my blood with sharp lancet

Satisfied, she waits for me to finish.
But my horn she had overlooked
Which I blew upon to summon a friend
Who brings me my great bow.
It defies her with an arrow
Shooting up & far over my forest
To where I must be buried
There to grow again:
New forest, new merry ways, new story.

(z)
After my music lesson
Three miles
Through
The Stream
Of Wind
And of Wet
Tonight
I walk and walk
Till Home at last
By Stove, Hot Water, Tub,
Supper,
Drowsy listening to Radio,
Mother, Homework, Bed —
There the grateful stream of Sleep
Slides in and under
The other Stream outside
Still flowing Ice and Rain.

ACKNOWLEDGEMENTS

Poems in this collection have appeared previously.

Caroline H. Davidson
Canadian Author & Bookman, Poetry Toronto, Rufus, Strong Winds, Wordscape 2.

Sonja Dunn
Aquarius, Butterscotch Dreams (Pembroke Pub.), The Northern Poet, Tide Pool (Hamilton Haiku Press), Spring Fever.

Bernice Lever
Mix Six (Mekler & Deahl), Spring Fever, Things Unsaid (Black Moss), Writer's Block.

Roger Nash
Antigonish Review, Fiddlehead, Malahat Review, More Garden Varieties Two, Parchment.

James Reaney
Windsor Review, The LCP Museletter.

Robert Sward
Mississippi Review, Saturday Review, The Hudson Review, The Paris Review.